Elegies from

New York City

Elegies from

New York City

Mirela Roznoveanu

[KOJA PRESS]

New York · 2008

Elegies from New York City

First Edition

ISBN-10: 0-9773698-4-6
ISBN-13: 978-0-9773698-4-3

Library of Congress Control Number: 2007940395

Copy Editor: William James Austin
Cover design: Igor Satanovsky
Front cover artwork: *Ballerina's Dream (3)*, from the tryptic painting *Ballerina's Dream* by Razvan Neicu (1945-2005)

Printed in the United States of America

Koja Press books are distributed by
SPD/ Small Press Distribution, Berkeley, CA

For more information about Koja Press, visit our Web site
http://kojapress.com

The following poems have been translated
from the Romanian by Heathrow O'Hare:

Continuum;
Loneliness in New York City;
The Design of Fate;
The Strait Gate;
Of Times Immemorial;
October Night;
December Night;
February Night;
A Night in March;
September.

CONTENTS

New York Elegies

From East to West

Nights

I

NEW YORK ELEGIES

MY LEGEND [1]

I am told that some people detest me
because I dared escape the dullness
of an anonymous life
                    through inner narcosis.

My real condition is as follows:
          Biology's overwhelming the spirit;
          all deadlines are irrelevant;
          actually, I have decided
          to give up setting myself any more deadlines.

Biology has taken over;
leisurely surveying this plowed acre,
its rows of carefully tended literary projects –
dormant seeds –
with no time limit set for the blooming stage;
postponing spring indefinitely;
hardly able to drag my shattered body along.

Blessed be whatever induces anesthesia,
such as sleeping potions and pills,
or my brain's endorphins, while I'm writing –
my inner narcosis.

The reality principle:
          I sometimes take pains
          to get myself some anesthesia;
          the deeper, the better.
                    [After having some surgery
                    I went to a Brazilian restaurant

– blood over my anesthesia –
and had black beans and *capirinha de
cachaça*, stronger than *palinca*,
the twice distilled
Romanian plum brandy;
– blood all over my mouth –
and that amazing *cachaça* numbing
whatever was live in my soul]

I remember my mother's sleeping pills
by the side of her bed—
disgusted by my father infidelities
she left the bedroom and him in it
and moved into a tiny sanctum
at the corner of the house—
she was about forty-five when she started sleeping alone;
thorny those nights as she was still trying
to keep track of my father's late
to-ings and fro-ings.

What a blessing to get a bit of anesthesia,
or have one's soul distracted by fever,
or by potions that suspend one's sense of mind and body!

The real thing:
          A man's aware but of the woman
he lies in bed with,
          all others – mere events of his imagination.

The imagination is cold –
Memories, chilly.

I actually live in opposition to what I've just said.

I'm aware of whatever's happening,
or is about to happen;
I can perceive other people's
thoughts and feelings.
With the same intensity –
as if they were occurring right now –
I can relive events of the distant past;

I can see through walls;
I know the things which I didn't wish to accomplish,
and whatever exists, far away,
lies right by my side.

The real thing:
          More potions blocking the monstrous sensitivity
                              that comes with the package –
                                        the poet's gift.

                    I'm all things –
                    Everything's me –

                    I—the Daemon.

ANOTHER SPRING

In the shade of trees—
dressed up like Arthur's knights
magnificently celebrating my arrival, —
I, their Queen,
whom they would all die fighting for,
sob on from the depth of my smarting sides.
They tremble in their crisp membranes,
useless vegetable armors,
ready to provide relief to my anguish.

I have gloriously survived one more winter.
Desperations bloom again in May –
bordering the purple round table in the courtyard
with marjoram.

The sun is melting down the ice
which kept darkness quiet in my heart.

Trees with foliage
the color of a bull's blood
pollinate my thoughts,
which mourn the throbbing of my own blood.

THE BASEBALL FIELD

is surrounded by the highway
connecting Queens and Brooklyn,
two 'Car and Wash' shops',
the cemetery, the children's playground,
and the electric plant.

On a mid-August day at 3 P.M., the wind blowing
                                       yellow dust all over,
the ballgame's being watched
by two mothers
and by God,
both under the attack
of the same ruthless sun and both prepared
to lend a meaning to it all.

The players' pledge that
Royals and *Panthers* will work it out.
The noise comes from the highway traffic
and the wind
and, once in a while, a mother's voice: *Go, go!* –
and God's indistinct whisper . . .

Nobody in the field is speaking to anyone;
players change roles and faraway spots:
the one that throws the ball gazes
at the triangular white stone
and dutifully polishes it.
Stray seagulls holler in the sky.
The player about to hit the ball
incessantly swings the silvery club;
the one that is to catch it

waits stock-still with an iron mask.

All others sit on the side benches
or all over in the field waiting
for something that fails to happen
and when it does
its speed is beyond my eyes capacity to follow.
The only noticeable thing's the point of death —
the touching of the white stone — the base.

It is like nobody's doing anything
for hours in that field —
some move from one spot to another
in slow motion.
The ball is in or out.
There are no orders or commands
and the game goes on for hours
while the tensions remain unexpressed.
And the moves are so rash
and of such uncertain rigor,
and their structure
barely visible,
with rules so hard to comprehend
for an outsider.
No emotions;
nobody seems to lose or win
and all of a sudden the game comes to an ending.
There is a winner, yet I can't discover who.

My American life.

THE BLACK BIRD

The wind is waving the myriads of shiny green leaves.
The fragrance of mown grass takes the field over,
flooding the Universe with its living vegetable moisture.

I am a black bird dwelling in this lofty tree hollow.
The tree is my love as I am his.
Divided by the different planes of existence,
we are unable to share a lot.
Yet, I am happy to sleep in his arms -

THE NEW ORPHEUS

The abyss grows deeper and deeper
each time you glance back,
sang Orpheus as the rabid bitches tore him up.

Remember how I lost Eurydice;
how the path leading to life,
as flimsy as the spider's
insubstantial passage,
would vanish at the slightest doubt.

Beware walking the Inferno's ridges
for the abyss is waiting to swallow you up;
you're feeding it
while gazing down into it.

THE FELICIFIC CALCULUS

The years ahead
are fewer than those left behind—
by such a computation I whiled my time away
                    during my last insomnia.
And what a relief in the morning,
in the crowded subway car
riding to my office!

I'll go through fewer desperate moments
fewer disappointments
fewer betrayals
fewer sleepless nights
fewer humiliations
fewer worries
fewer tears
fewer struggles.

Happiness cannot grow less—
less than what's so tiny already.

I'm looking forward to being cheerful and joyful.

Calculus of this kind always makes you feel right.

CONTINUUM

The Romanian past will not decay in New York,
nor will it prove overwhelming.
It is arrested in the Present Tense
liberating the future, thus.

In New York, the immigrant's past, irrespective
                                  of his or her culture,
has no bearing on the present
for there is a different kind of present here,
which is called *continuous*
and which has no counterpart in Romanian or in Spanish,
            wherever they may be spoken, nor in Japanese.
The same is true of the Future Continuous Tense.

The American tenses wash out the past tenses of the
recently arrived to the point of oblivion;
memory takes refuge in dreams
allowing the-here-and-the-now freedom of choice.

In the gods' privileged temporal continuum
only the sound of words
is as important as their meaning.
Tenses and thoughts are not beholden to reality
as they are not a substantial part of it
only a hyperbolic sign
        of the infinite sets
among the many more of the universe.

In the tumult of the temporal continuum

the newcomer experiences
a self-annihilating work frenzy
                and delight *ad nauseam.*

Thinking him- or herself all-powerful in the chimera
                of the temporal continuum –
which will eventually take each of them piecemeal apart –
to the gods' irrepressible cheer.

ARRACACHA

The golden root of the Chibchas
reached me in New York City on a hot afternoon
like a message from the native Indians of Colombia
on how to expose
the secret torments of our lives
on pine stakes.

Arracacha is a root that looks
like a spearhead on my plate.

I eat it boiled
as a necessary sweet spike
following the withdrawal of needles from my body.

Needles all over my body every afternoon—
I need them more and more
to cope with the inner heartache.
Needles inserted into the crown of my head,
pricking my brow and all the way
along the middle of my chest
and belly,
my arms and hands,
my legs and ankles,
my soles and my toes.

Life becomes easier after the shock of piercing—
I can breathe for a few hours,
released from the agony of solitude.

I can go ahead in time.

As my tears soak the pillow
on the acupuncturist's treatment table,
they drip to the floor and so
trickle down into the soil,
feeding the Colombian golden arracacha.

THE AMAZONIAN PRINCIPLE

"Go away from him or murder him
after the first night of lovemaking.
If you cannot, do it after the second or the third.
Beware; you will not be able to do it
after the fourth one
for you will be taken over" –
said the voice of the last woman warrior
                                    from Scythia,
slaughtered in my dream by her lover
                                    during their fifth night.
The Amazonian message was supposedly buried;
mankind did not need it.
It unexpectedly surfaced in New York's temporal vortex.

"Making love to him, you lose your power;
his brain will take over yours,
his sweetness will possess every bit of yourself
—the whispers went on coming from nowhere—
tearing a path in your body
for all those who will follow.
You won't be able to see the real he anymore,
but rather what he will wish you to see.
His desires will override yours,
his blood will run in your veins,
his wishes will become a dream for you to fulfill,
and you will call all of this love
while it is but your submission
to the venom slowly poisoning you,
transforming you into a slave,
running your life through the fear
that one day you will lose him

to another woman,
which is anyway bound to happen.
Try to find out at least who deserves this sacrifice
demanded by the law of the species.
Powerful women keep their distance
from the ones they really love;
they know that loneliness does not exist."

      I was already awake – I, a woman
      from Scythia Minor –
sensing the perfume of another woman,
amused by her *alternate presence*,
embarrassed by all those nights that had happened.
I did not quite understand
why he was by my side,
      his breath reeking of spirits,
      his soul resembling that of a brute,
      his mind no more than that of a beast.

I snatched my spear and my shield
and slaughtered him methodically in my soul,
releasing that unwanted poison from my being,
getting myself ready for the next challenge of tomorrow.

IN THE AMETHYST CAVE

I was speeding through Skylla and Charybdis,
like Ulysses,
all through this bitter and blooming world.

My native land was a perfect amethyst egg
wrapped in its dusty-green shell
like a sarcophagus of the Menopus era
still in the Egyptian desert
with no one unlocking its ancient door to freedom
though the cursed 40 or 400 or 4000 years are gone.
No Moses yet.

Here in New York, as in a nightmare, I keep recalling
bits of a Skylla and Charybdis' *Decalogue,*
glistening all over my frightened skinny frame,
daily poisoned to the very last gasp of Death –
an incantation in the promiscuous lyricism of Romanian,
(oh, Romanian's self-destructive hospitality!)

Skylla and *Charybdis*:
Do not independently think;
do but what you've been told to.
We will always take care of you
And do not let yourselves be terrified by the death kit,
For you'll lie here with us in the ground -- an everlasting
lump of shit.

Skylla:
Be calm and report to me whatever you hear or see;
Round up those traitors conspiring against me.

Charybdis:
Don't trust anybody, whether lovers or family;
they are my confidential informers, daily reporting to me.

Skylla:
Hate your desires, also your close friends;
Hate your self-denials, your vital inclinations.

Charybdis:
Freedom is granted to you only because we need you
for our comfort;
The outside world is of the craziest sort.

Skylla:
Crush whoever's doing more than you do;
And force him to behave the way he has been taught to.

Skylla and Charybdis:
Indulge in gossip; give up the interest
in self-preservation; when hard-pressed,
write to show your scorn towards all foreigners:
they are our country's enemy -- both inner and outer.

One day I closed my ears tight,
my eyes, the pores of my skin --
living out my lot inside Skylla and Charybdis's camp
and I saw my crucified mind!
Sunlight flooded my awareness
of my paralyzed state;
I could sense the oppressive air of a jail;
I saw myself lying handcuffed
on the amethyst floor --
an offering to barbarous idols.

I no longer needed proofs
to summon the courage to get out
of the sorceresses' cave.

I felt guilty for having tried, over the years,
to forget my mother tongue intoxicated by witches' songs.

Sometime I feel like building a blank wall
inside my memory
so that behind it I might rediscover
the gentleness of Romanian.
But will I succeed, with Skylla and Charybdis still there?

BATTERING THE PEAR TREE

Only the fruit-bearing trees get battered.
It hurts. But who cares about the barren ones?

When it is almost ripe with branches bending
under fruit in the fall of mature ideas
thieves arrive to steal the harvest.

Bearing fruit hurts.
Thieves' sneaky aggression springs
from their painful obsession with impotence
and unfinished projects.

The pear tree considers thieves
as dandelion seeds blown all over.
Why should I be upset, the tree muses?
Thieves spread my essence around.
Who cares under whose name it gets known?

Whenever the fruit is ripe and ready for picking
the pear tree is shaken and battered.
It is mean of the thieves to aim stones high at its canopy.

The pear tree thinks of those vandals with compassion:
Why should I be upset? The pear tree muses.
Only fruit bearing trees are shaken and thrashed.
Who cares about the barren ones?

Thieves are climbing my trunk and limbs,
greedy to get what I've dearly grown ever since the spring,
and I let them do it in pain and relief.

LONELINESS IN NEW YORK CITY

I've reached the point of praying that friends
      be no more taken from me.
I light a candle at six in the morning and talk
                  to Her
– the one who in the icon reads from the Book –
very much like her Son.
We two are both alone: She reading, I trying hard
to make Her say "Good morning!" to me.

In the summer-heated city, the ocean's vapors
fail to thaw even the thinmost crust
                  of the ice floes,
as they drift down from the North Pole of Souls.
People speak in discrete short syllables,
smiling shyly, defending, as it were, their armor
beneath which new icy layers get formed.
Feelings are allowed only when they reach the lowest
                  heating threshold.

Each practices self-defense from everybody else;
no one is willing to get close to any one;
the preservation of the icy crust is vital
at the North Pole of Souls.

Afflictions are quickly frozen
(Ah, those wonderfully colored pills, people jogging,
fitness clubs!)
passions bound in chains – *She's a silly Romanian
enthusiast* – I'm constantly hearing this kind of remark.
The ice-clad people walk along paths that

would never cross, and when detours occur
they turn for help to the 'managers of souls.'

Raphael, the Angel, descends as *Eau de Cologne*,
available on Fifth Avenue.

So mightily do the ice floes sparkle
that whole battalions of souls from all continents
are willing to get crushed only to be able to touch them.

Morgan le Fay of the North Pole of Souls
displays her breath-taking splendor.
The imperfect ones, who resist being iced over,
will slowly die,
happily dreaming,
ranting love soliloquies
inside superbly fitted-out madhouses.

GROWING OLD

God invented senility, sickness, and madness
to help people sever relationships before death
and those surviving to say good-bye to them.

> Craving death as a blessing,
>   craving it as a relief.

Families hiding the secret of crushed love
in remote locked rooms
(it is the way parents
protect their young against their grandparents' rage
tainting the air around).
My mother's cousin was kept in a remote room
where no food was allowed.

> Craving death as a blessing,
>   craving it as a relief.

They say they know
how to make husbands and wives hate each other,
sons despise their parents
relatives turn into enemies for the rest of their lives.

> Craving death as a blessing,
>   craving it as a relief.

Scriptures say let the living be with the living
the dead with the dead,
the sick with the sick
the old ones with the old.

Craving death as a blessing,
craving it as a relief.

It is not the panic confronting death;
it is the revulsion of seeing creatures freed from death, at
least for a while.
Piercing the others—
the devastating effects of their presence,
the way to stay alive
and there's no pity here.

Craving death as a blessing,
craving it as a relief.

In my mother's Macedo-Romanian tribe
from the Pindus Mountains
the widower was allowed to remarry and survive;
the widow was confined to the dark loneliness
and neglect for the remainder of her life,
unless she had the decency of dying
soon – her undeniable proof of love.

NEW YORK

1.
Perfection and seduction are its names.
The paradigmatic city of my world
gives birth to its mythology every morning.

Humans seem tolerated exceptions
to the well-organized beauty.

Here is the place where everything works,
where everything on earth exists,
where people do not cry for food,
for freedom, for comfort, for jobs,
but for things unthinkable in other places
such as 'loneliness,' 'friends,' 'closeness'...

Hordes of disposable human beings fuel
with their fresh energy
the secret furnaces of the city.

They come for money and freedom
and the city gives them as much as they can get.

2.
You must be really happy to be here,
in the most perfect place that
humanity has conceived in its history.
It's a place built by people
brought over from across the ocean,
and after that by the Irish tormented by famine,

and by the Chinese who built
the East River subway tunnels.
And by you.

You are welcome, though, to experience it on your skin.
It will be only an experience
if you know how to get out of it
for in coming here you have utterly lost
the place you left behind.

3.
It is the perfect city on earth, the shining star
hardly known by immigrants living
                              in Queens, the Bronx,
and Brooklyn, or Staten Island,
shuttling underground to and from work
by the subway.
You cannot see them in the city,
flooded by tourists and corporate or white-collar clerks
having lunch in Midtown or in Downtown.
New immigrants eat their lunch brought from home.
They save every penny
dreaming the American Dream.
They are lucky if they have families
(and cursed if they don't)
in the city on whose streets people
                              speak to themselves aloud.

The 21st century postmodern pyramids
                    of greed are fueled
                    by antidepressants
and lithium and by its generic drugs.
Fear and loneliness flow
on the shinning surfaces

polished by the invisible blood,
which is all over as part
of the shinning facades.
There is greater loneliness in the crowded city
than in the jungle.

4.
The Aztec and Mayan gory rituals
                    have been preserved all over.
The pre-Columbians passed them all down to us.
They are in the air and the soil.
They've been absorbed by the settlers
                    with their daily meals,
despite the disappearance of the Mayans and the Aztecs
and of many other pre-Columbian peoples.

The New Modern Age pyramids
are fueled by the same old cruelty.
Yet you don't see priests snatching the heart
                    from their victims' chest.
You can only see perfection, rules and regulations,
managers regulating your words and feelings,
efficiency and expertise and competition
to the very limit and beyond of human endurance.

In the greatest city in the world
life is analyzed and watched
by teams of security guards
in charge with your safety and productivity,
spelled out in monthly reports of your calls, moves,
breathing, laughs and smiles,
suicidal thoughts.
You are safe and clean.
It is in your best interest.

5.
Life is so private;
nobody asks anything.
Nobody calls over the weekend for privacy reasons.
Caller IDs protect everybody from one another.

Privacy is respected and valuable.
If one cries nobody looks at his or her face,
if one does not sleep the entire night
and desperation flows in and out of his or her eyes,
(s)he is asked: "Are you OK?"
If you are not, go home, you will not be paid for this day,
sorry,
for you endanger the productivity
              efficiency
                    perfection.

Privacy is respected
nobody asks anything
all questions are job related
and answers should be focused.
Do not deviate from the tiny point of the question.
Otherwise you are told you are "all over"
and this goes into your file
in the Manager's drawer.

6.
FOCUS.
To the point of nonbeing.
Tutorials and 'how to' guides

will instruct you how to walk at your workplace
how to move your lips
how smiling is important while you answer questions
and what happens if you do the opposite—
'clean your desk' is the magic phrase
when a human being gets discarded.

7.
It is the city of the young and energetic ones
                              easily seduced
whose blood can fuel the city's furnaces.
The old ones have to go
to faraway compounds built for elderly people
in the middle of nowhere
in wagon houses of those squeezed
by small pensions
that are a burden for their busy children
struggling in the city's furnaces.
These are the lucky ones
still on their feet,
for the others are jailed in home care facilities
losing anything they had – from dignity to freedom –
their money and the lovely memories of their lives.

God, look at the nursing homes
fortified by lines of guards on duty
where the old fellow is a prisoner
                    until death comes as a relief
where he or she has to ask for permission
to step out on the street to get a mouthful of fresh air,
not the air conditioning, and see the real sky,

not the one through windows that filter the light– devices
fastened to their hands or feet would start the alarm in
case the main entrance door has been opened –

You have to have the permission there
                              to open a window –
as the latter is locked for security reasons –
you have to ask the permission to be a human being,
while watched by hidden cameras,
fed at the right hours with the right medication,
told what to do – for you've lost the right
to think, judge, and decide on your own –
sedated with tranquilizers if questions arise
and sent to the hospital in a hurry when near death
as nursing homes would not gladly suffer their inmates
die in their beds.

And the smell of urine is all over,
and humans as vegetables in wheelchairs,
with wrists bands provided with alarm devices
and coldness keeping alive those squeezed bodies
but not their minds.

It is the place where the elderly give up all their rights
through 'the power of attorney'
and guardians decide to vacate their homes
hold their wedding bands
give them a dollar for a soda
for they have no needs and judgment and desires.
This is the exit door
for those not useful
                              for the city's furnaces anymore.

8.
It is called the Big Apple
with some likely connotations
from the forbidden Apple of seduction, as well.

I see it as an iron sphere or iron apple,
                                    not the golden one,
where no one enters or exits at will.

You cannot enter the Big Apple
by just walking in on the road.
The Big Apple is a citadel
                connected with the outside
through tunnels, highways, and bridges,
watched and guarded at entrances and exits.

You cannot just walk into the Apple
entering the iron doors;
you cannot just walk into the sphere
for you need to buy a ticket for it.
The same is true of the exit.

You have to pay for breathing its air
and by walking into the Iron Sphere you feed it.
And always give more than you get—
this is the rate of exchange, in here.

It is shinning as a lighthouse
            and the desperate ones from all continents get the
                                    shining message,
                                        marching to it,
wishing to feed the Apple's thrust
for the fresh essences of life.
There shall never be enough lured hordes

to feed the hungry Iron Apple of seduction.

Humans seem tolerated exceptions
to the well-organized beauty.

The paradigmatic city of my world
gives birth to its mythology every morning.

THE DESIGN OF FATE

is like a fabric simultaneously woven
by several persons in different places,
each altering her pattern with respect to the model
                          developed by the others –
and that's why it is incommensurate.
Could this be the way the Moira are acting,
the nice young ladies **of destiny**
who have fun improvising
variations on eternal themes and motifs
betting on the note upon which the gods' soul will
implode as will the flesh
of those entrusted to them by the gods?

If nothing is eternal in the universe,
not even death as such,
do we experience non-death cyclically?

Each book I have written is a cosmic object traveling
its own path. How far will it reach?

Some are drawn to each other by their plainness,
others are separated by their beauty.
Take me, Angel, I've pleaded in my dream,
and she answered me: Do you think it would be
such an easy matter after all you've built up here?

THE STRAIT GATE

For Liliana Ursu

To move across America astride an illusion
mounted between two humps –
                              the past and the present –
my son glances over his shoulder and smiles at me:
"What are you up to Mother?"
"I'm trying to get born again
and to give birth to you, as well."
"I, too, am waiting to get born again."

In Mirela's home an invisible sacred fire
is burning.

Maximilian asks for a sheet of paper,
Dan tries to spell out
the most beautiful and strange map:
Mirela's sole.

New York City is sprawling out of doors.
Indoors we huddle together – the old friends,
and Bucharest's Rahova and Cotroceni districts,
and the computer that whispers to us tenderly:
the keys tapped by Mihnea and by Maximilian
trying to express something in Romanian.

Too many things have happened today
                              in my tumultuous life;
I feel like this gadget that probably knows everything,
yet it can still learn something
from a child who goes through a period

that is difficult and at the same time extraordinary,
a period in which he's going to receive
                              the very first true kiss.

Then said one unto him, 'Lord, are there few that be
saved?'
And he said unto them,
            'Strive to enter in at the strait gate: for many, I
                                        say unto you,
    will seek to enter in, and shall not be able.'

MY LEGEND [2]

I've been told to give up long sentences.
In order to succeed, I'll have to forget the convoluted
turns and counterturns of Romance languages.

The same cadence over and over:
                              subject, predicate, object.
A soldier's beat *ad nauseam*.

I'm fifty five.
Only my brain keeps menstruating.
I'm still a woman.
But I'm a man too.
Twice I have dreamed of possessing a woman.

Having to be alone in the room while I write.
Men only in faraway rooms should be allowed.

I went to India following in the footsteps
                              of Alexander the Great.
I realized why he had gone there:
to bathe in the eternal light,
still there over the Ganges in Varanasi
waiting for me.

It is springtide now.
I burned all my diaries at 21.
I feel like doing the same.

My friends. My Homer.
My teachers. My Socrates.

My body – my Goethe.

I feel like smoking, yet I can't.
I feel like drinking, yet all I get is a heartburn.
I do not use underwear in the summer
"to fight the witches' curses" – a Romanian saying.

Somehow the loneliness of the rainforest –
that's what I'm experiencing during weekends
in New York City.
A man from Europe I lived with for a while had a mistress
back there.
When he got drunk, he spoke about her.
He asked me to love her.
I asked him to ask her to love me too.
I am not sure whether in me he saw his faraway mistress.

Orgasms during nighttime while dreaming.
The best ever.
And also in early puberty
not knowing what was happening
while sleeping in secret chambers carpeted with
handmade rugs
and filled with barrels of salty tasty feta cheese.
Many times I found drowned lizards in those barrels.
The cheese acquired a distinctive tang.
The same with the pickle in other barrels.

Having to be alone in the room while I write.
Men only in faraway rooms should be allowed.

Cooking apple pies,
I am thinking of Jason's golden apples.
I am very fond of him.

Peeling the apples I see Jason stealing them.
I was doing the same with quinces in my
childhood. Did Jason eat those apples?
Yet I keep seeing him stealing those golden apples.

Drifting through this endless emptiness of my life, I write
poems while thinking of writing poems. The art of poetry.

> I write poetry once every ten years. Prowling like a
> beast in search of myself.

I had been here before I was born.
I had been perceived before my existence.

My Legend [2] Footnote 1: *Shamanlike*

memories of the other
escalating a self-destructive behavior
she eats hurriedly and
rudely
she cannot slow down
bulimia
eating without tasting
early years of promiscuity
an effort to define herself through victimization?

Self-inflicted
psychical wounds.

Something shamanlike in her
thinking about her
obsessively
her sexual power
old gods descend
in the body
of the chosen woman.

My Legend [2] Footnote 2: *Cosmetics*

Beauty and its distance
from reality.

Cosmetics covering over
of the real.

Consciousness in alert---
fissure between self and
face and body
as perceived by others:

not an ideal but
an effect.

My Legend [2] Footnote 3: *Sophronian Chant*

Healing a few of the remaining earthlings
of misunderstanding
of the failure of vision
of the gap between meaning and sign

Cherubical hymn

significance

signification

poetry fakes

the disappearance of sense and substance

sterilized images

counterfeit

error

Angelic

inaccurate names faring much better with time
the antithetical one
that is adequate in a different conceptual system

myself attracting madmen

Sophronian Chant – a soothing one of healing powers...

I've asked the prophetess CK in Sedona
why am I getting on with this mess
and her answer was: "because of your *sophronian* voice"

II

FROM EAST TO WEST

MEDITATION ON A FRENCH BROTHEL

Indian summer on the fifth floor terrace in bloom
suffused by the millennium-old sunshine exercises
                                                    over Paris

life has acquired new meanings
words and time compounded together

> Each day is just like another man
> Each word is just like another customer
> and I – the prostitute
> **Who's paying who?**

> Words blossoming on the terrace
> of the former brothel in Paris
> roundabout *les Halles*
> on the fifth floor on *rue du Cygne*
> with *rue Saint Dennis*
> of the *Saint Leu - Saint Gilles Cathedral*

> **Is verbena the odor of grace?**

> Time units do foolish things in the organ of the
> nearby *Notre Dame de Paris*
> Past and present and future hiss
> in verbal units   broken images cavalcade
>   in the candlelight's flare
> the siege of outside darkness is the midnight's real

> **Do the guardian gargoyles scream
> against the demons or at myself?**

I gargoyle?

Time gargoyles?

cymbals drums in outbursts
Time sells its music
Tube tones
Crushing pitch of low-end thunder
Time's engine   a massive crunch   unleashes
the fury

The former brothel building and the cathedral
facing each other
echoing connotations
subtexts
overtones

I see no difference between myself
and Lilly the eighty years old whore
on *rue du Cygne*
we deal graciously with our customers
mine are words & time –
light turns green or red in her windows
depending on how busy she is –
I'm learning to deal with such signs
while climbing the narrow green-carpeted stairs to the
red fifth floor

My soul's foliage is trembling all over

as the sun sinks behind the rooftops of Paris
while brothel and cathedral mirror
the doves in broken stained-glass windows

Here on the fifth floor I feel dominated
by men
by time
by   my own words

Might there be a different meaning for affection?

Remarkable words bloom on the terrace of the former
brothel mirroring the cathedral

Look at every word's pointed arch
Sense the words tentacles as the cathedrals' arches point
to the infinite
Inhale the words various meanings--
a multitude of meanings within the cathedral's arches

At least some of them can be seen

**How many others have been driven underground
or over the rooftops?**

The gargoyles are watching over
the meanings

They preserve the inner labyrinth

of words
poems

cathedrals

Labyrinth – the longest path on the shortest
possible unit of space
as the pilgrimage to the
center of soul and grace

Time units -- as verbal units while I write   exist
compose

Gargoyles   defend   me   and   my   writing

time units

implode

into

words

WALKING THE FREEDOM TRAIL

At noon in early July, 2004 –
I'm taking the year 1634 on the soles of my feet
across the Boston Common,
under its blossoming linden trees.

(The nearby Granary Burial Ground
is filled with the wailing of the Massacre
of March 5, 1770.
The nation's 4th of July is but a couple of years away)

Many of the events and decisions, taken in
critical times
and related to my immigrant experience,
I've fully understood only of late.

What's your truth, Mr. Samuel Adams, and yours,
       Mr. John Hancock,
and yours, Mr. Peter Faneuil, and yours,
       Mr. Paul Revere,
that you have been resting here
    in the Granary Burial Ground,
in the soil of the grain storage building
turned into the granary of freedom?

(It is such an honor to be talking with you,
and thereby grasp what made you successful
       in your Revolution,
while I have failed in mine)

Tremont bordering Boston Common
and the Freedom Trail,
the Granary Burial Ground of the revolutionaries
who shaped America, while my country's future
was abandoned to those whom the Revolution
had in vain tried to topple from History's stage.

Let the thought of betrayal perish and with it
my habit to weigh the losses in my life,
as if I had always aimed at goals from behind
like an amnesiac or someone incapable of forgetting,
ridden by emotions and by guilt,
involving the grain storage buildings in my native land,
which have all failed as granaries of freedom.

I am lucky, though, to have succeeded in joining
my thinking self to the heart
of the American granary burial grounds,
allowing its unruly mane to race by the side
of those likewise engaged in wild pursuits
at a time of spiritual drought.

MONSOON

The mother cactus is pregnant
in Arizona's July magma.
Leaves roofed by spines
covered here and there
by orange uteri crammed with
black little kernels,
tucked safely into juicy vaults.
They dream of the rainy East,
not realizing their spines
              would be of no use there
and water would corrupt
              their unquenchable thirst.

I am not a cactus,
although I might have to become one
in order to survive on my way
from East to West.
Spines do not thoroughly cover my skin yet
and my thirst for a new universe is still unquenched.
The Monsoon's squalls frighten me
in the whistling desert.

I cannot be motionless like a cactus—
emotions surface despite the mimetic adherence
to the laws of survival in the desert.

And what is the desert?
A tract of land that once
              had gone through death throes,
a plot of mourning ground

showing indifference or hate
for nature's bounty.
It is like an abandoned lover–
like a wife who's husband died
or ran away with another woman–
        like one whose trust in love and life
            has been betrayed–
like a human being that lost
all of its kind.

The Monsoon arrives to heal the desert's wounds
bringing soothing, water, and shade
to the pitiless brightness of the dunes.
Hope envelops the pregnant cacti,
dangerously bonded in the airstreams,
overflown by the Arizonian forests'
lack of coolness.

The Monsoon brings the desert back to life
and my heart too–
as the abundant summer rains bring restoration
to the Romanian fertile plains.

My thorny skin shelters my emotions in the Arizonian
desert while my wavy flowing hair mixes
with the long palm leaves
beckoning from the Monsoon's roaring streams.
The convulsed groan of palm trees and philodendra
is so unlike the sweet sound of cute tiny
pine needles and the small leaves of the leafy trees
in the eastern forests of the Carpathian Mountains!

It takes a very special universe to make one happy.

MOTHER OF ALL BUTTERFLIES

All the fleshly parts lie inside;
hence the outer skeleton gets so easily broken—
My children cannot carry their armor
for too long.

I had been fortunate to wear my flesh
as a shield protecting my emotions.

Unable to heal from treacheries,
I've become sort of a Morpho butterfly, lately.
Its delicate flesh is shielded
by the outer skeleton, which breaks so easily.
All punches hurt
and my blue hues cannot blend
with the similar ones in my world.

I may well be a Mother of All Butterflies
feeding them with such sweets
like a banana slice on a plate.

I am quite a Morpho
with electric blue wings like most Morphos—
that cobalt of dreams brought about by Morpheus
and by infinity—
alighting only on things alike,
blending my outer skeleton
                against the selfsame flowers' hues
in order to take a break,
and put an end to the endlessly joyful fatigue of flapping.

The only way to find protection
is to get my blue emotions blended.

I am looking for similar hues
in order to relax them within the Morpho state,
but I've not encountered them in the garden
I'm flapping about.

ON THE CONVERSION FROM BEAST TO HUMAN

Ancient metamorphoses pointed to conversion
as to a form of exiling the human
to the animal, vegetable,
                    or mineral condition.

They spoke about the inferno of going
from higher to lower states of being.

It is the harshest punishment one can imagine,
turning a human being into a tree or an animal,
depriving it of the power to do magic, move,
                    and speak –
constraining it for ever to be a flower or a river,
although some ancient gods would resort to similar
transient changes
in their attempt at seducing mortals.
The human appearance for them
                    was a kind of a jail.
And sex was all they were after.

Metamorphoses tell us they are the only accepted way
of sudden change in our world,
from the higher to the lower.

I've tried elevation.
I took a beast into my house
and fed it with my own food.
I taught the beast to speak,
to be polite, to say "thank you,"

to trust and to be trustful.

I've always contradicted
and tested the wisdom of the universe
as well as that of long established meanings.

I wanted to see whether it worked in the West as well.
Could metamorphosis be a way of rewarding good deeds?

I was reluctant to recall the pagan story of the man
who having found a frozen serpent in the forest,
put it under his coat to keep it warm,
but the serpent bit him by way of being thankful.

While deeply absorbed into my world,
the beast sank its teeth into my jugular.
I was vulnerable, writing a poem at my desk,
a piece of work he could not suspect
                    what meaning it might have.

He looked happily at the blood streaming down my body.
The beast's ears kept moving the way
                    the wolves' do at slaughter,
          —you don't seem to have died,
          the beast said softly in the language learned
          from me,
          but you will—

THE STAGECOACH DRIVER

Driving a stagecoach loaded with passengers' baggage,
mail, and gold dust,
over the Sierra Nevada Mountains
during the 1850's, meant taking both danger and
hardship in your stride.
Charlie Parkhurst held this job
for nearly twenty years.
Being fierce and clever
the highwaymen did him in only twice.
The first time, he was caught unawares without a gun and
forced to hand down the money box.
The second time, he fired his shotgun
at the outlaw's chest and escaped.

(Express money, *Wells, Fargo and Co,*
Buffalo Bill, Butch Cassidy, and Billy the Kid,
all of them in Wells Fargo History Museum
on 145 W. Adams St. in Phoenix, Arizona,
where I met Charlie Parkhurst,
the stagecoach driver)

I liked Charlie's slim and wiry 5'6" figure,
his alert gray eyes, and shyness.
I instinctively sensed what he must have felt
while driving the stagecoach, dreaming there
on his seat of the purple horse-drawn carriage,
displayed at the museum.

He rarely smiled; his voice was shrill and high-pitched.
They said he never talked about himself

and loneliness was his only lover.
He had driven the stagecoach to the very end of the
1860's, through the mud and dust
of the Sierra Nevada Mountains.
They discovered when he died that, as a matter of fact, he
had been a woman, at some point in her life
becoming a mother.

It took me a long time to meet my sister Charlie
in the Wild, Wild West!
To be a female literary essayist
in the 1970's in the Wild, Wild East
was similar to becoming a stagecoach driver
in the Sierra Nevada Mountains in the 1850's.
It meant taking danger and hardship in one's stride.
And rejection.
They said a woman did not have a theoretical mind,
that she could not write literary criticism,
that a woman's domain was the syrup
of mellow 'poetic' confession,
for she only had a uterus, not a brain.

I, too, had to disguise as a man, at the beginning
of my literary career,
signing my columns for years with an M.
This was considered the abbreviation
                    of a male author's name.
I fought in my columns like Charlie,
this time with literary bandits
who thought I was an old disgusting guy,
cynical and unforgiving ...

When I was for the first time challenged
to show up for a literary fight,

I did not know all male strategies of warfare,
but the second time I was fully prepared and attacked and
routed those outlaws
                              off the literary domain.

One day, a literary bandit found out my whereabouts
and wanted to beat me up.
He opened the door of the room where I was sitting
at my desk in an office with many others, somewhere in a
faraway Romanian city,
and loudly called me by my last name.
He was a mountain of flaming flesh, drunk and angry;
he had traveled several hundred miles to get me;
he was ready for a direct confrontation
out there on the street—
for a duel between two 'honorable' men.

I accepted the challenge.
He looked disgusted at my slim 5'6" delicate body—
I was in my twenties looking like a teenager—
and called me by my last name.

I was proud of my first name too.
He learned about it out there on the street
and later inside a pub,
where I drank him under the table.
It was the price for being allowed the use of my full-
lettered first name, for becoming
a woman literary critic.

THE PHOENIX ASHES: AN ODE

Life is a struggle to achieve metamorphoses—
the ancient Greeks were fully aware of it.
The number of transformations you could afford
is your answer to eternity.

Every morning you can feel the mystical
scent of the Phoenix being reborn.
Don't miss it!
Let yourself turn to ashes in the evenings,
to experience mortality;
and allow yourself to be reborn in the mornings,
to get the savor of eternity.
Keep within the Phoenix's shadow,
close to her western burning place,
so that your ashes might commingle with hers.
Otherwise you will miss your next morning rebirth,
as you might miss a highway exit
and get anywhere else, but back to life.

From the beginning of time,
the Phoenix would fly all the way west
to Arizona's Sonoran Desert, where
every evening she would burn itself to ashes.
She felt exhausted and was ready to burn.
Her aquamarine, white-irised eyes – large as cart-wheels
– used to scan every stone of the reddish mountains,
perceive every star, and all the coyotes and
rattle snakes lying hidden in the desert's cracks.
She knew, she suffered, and she yearned for peace.

Her purple plumes would wait for the final holocaust
in the Valley of the Sun with its burning sand,
yielding more color to the drab desert,
and enabling the few blooming sprigs of verbena
to maintain their flush.

I was fading in the Sonoran Desert's
heavenly light,
tired, yet ready to burst into flames,
looking for my cremation place
amongst the many mountains and their dazzling valleys.

Sadness and sorrow were my cardinal points.
Tossing upon the desert floor, already ashes,
my mind and soul
were carried in an urn by my dead-beaten body,
all the way to the West, where I would meet Her.

We bathed together in an oasis pond,
and sipped the last drops of earth's bounty.
Then the Phoenix allowed me to climb up
to the sacrificial spot
where flames would mix our ashes together—
a bird and a woman who,
equally exhausted, had come from East's farthest outpost
all the way to the West.

It was the Phoenix being reborn
from her ashes at sunrise
and my own self too, on the East Coast,
at my desk, where I use to write in the mornings,
my forehead hosting a Phoenix-like aquamarine eyes, the
fresh emptiness of my mind and soul ready to be filled.

I did know the way down to the Sonoran Desert,
where the Phoenix dies and comes back to life.
I did pass away in the Sonoran Desert.
I did come with my deserted soul to gaze on the desert.

I was only a corpse when I arrived
at the Sonoran Desert again, in the evening,
carrying the ashes of my mind and soul in an urn,
heading towards the burial spot into a saguaro shade.
I had spent the day submitting myself
to the craziest tasks and trials,
ready for the evening twilight, for the mountains,
and the cacti, and the dunes covered by brambles,
cooked in the desert's ovens,
with numbness and sadness my cardinal points.

We commingled our ashes again—as we shall do
many times from now on,
I can't say how often;
it depends on my speed in joining her
in the West, in the evenings—
and on my eyes, left in the morning with her,
as her eyes became mine,
while vanishing eastward into the sunrise.

I am the Phoenix Woman now,
with aquamarine eyes, white irises, purple hair,
preparing to enter evening, having flown all the way
from East to West
to get born from my ashes,
in a gust of wind,
tomorrow morning, before the sand catches fire
in the blissful light of the Sonoran Desert.

WETLANDS

There are pieces of unknown,
undiscovered parts of your essence,
similar to the Wokadahatchee swamp
right in the middle of the town.

An Anhinga with opened wings
                in the stillness of noon
rests in every one
as a black flag of sorrow;
turtles here and there exhibit their motionlessness
allergic to change
as well as alligators willing to get anything
in their apparent dream;
southern winds are whipping sand against your legs,
stirring up pieces of forgetfulness.

Dogs sleep in a deep embrace
on the sidewalks of South Miami Beach.
Every dog can hug here another dog,
yet no two people, a man and a woman.

Hurricanes reveal
the remembrance of an unheard-of song,
adjusting all sensations to a musical key
that fine-tunes all the musical scores in yourself.

You did not know what had been embedded
in the counterpoint of your shell,
you will hear your flesh singing,
all senses in tune to the same point,

the hidden musical spot of life.
South hot winds, awakenings
of the forgotten music of flesh.
Green, orange, and red days
as a palm fruit on the way to its ripeness—
the only adornment of neat trunks
      stormed over
            by the vicious metaphysic of existence.

OF TIMES IMMEMORIAL

Still standing there,
ever since before Noah and the continental drift,
the Hercynian range of the Macin Mountains
are patiently waiting for me in Dobrudja.
The Flood did not touch them –
the Danube obeyed them, changing its course –
the Black Sea shaped the contour of its shores
according to their wish –
the Carpathian Mountains bent themselves
under their occult guidance –
the Celts and the Thracians buried their kings
in tumuli at the feet of the Hercynian range –
the Romans admired them building Trajan's Wall
with rocks from their sides –
and somewhat earlier,
                    the Greeks had fled their harsh winters
leaving them the city states of Histria and Tomis
                                    as a parting gift.

Only my bosom friend Ovid
          would haunt them in springtime,
committing to memory, in the Hercynian languages,
the names of flowers, birds, or his *tristia*.

Clusters of hanging flowers brighten
                              the locust trees,
chamomile carpets fling out all their fragrance,
purple campanulas edge out of the lush
                    grasses of a purplish green,

while the red poppy hosts are keeping watch over oats
and wheat fields,
over the burial grounds where Father and Grandma were
laid to rest,
over the grazing herds of cattle,
and over me – the stray one.

I can gather my strength
only from my Hercynian ancestors,
worn-out, blunt, teeming with lizards,
– we, of times immemorial,
            speaking our secret languages –
amongst wild flowers,
            bathing in the primeval light
that's still surrounding the earth,
                  shielding the living,
and in the waves of fragrance yielded by these hills,
which once looked Himalayan.

The ALAMO, or the Unvanquished

In the Cavalry Courtyard of the Alamo Mission
I learn about those thirteen days in 1836
– the fighting between the Revolutionaries
                      and the Royalists –
and the struggle against overwhelming odds
of those men making the ultimate sacrifice
in defending the Republic of Texas.

William B. Travis, the commander of the Alamo Mission,
died on March 6, 1836
with all his friends and soldiers by sunrise
in the Mexican's siege led by General Santa Ana.
Travis loved poems. A book of poetry
that belonged to him
is displayed on his death's site.

If killed, silenced, or forced to leave
the site of your battle for freedom,
it does not necessarily mean
        that you've lost that battle.
El Alamo's thirteen days in 1836 spell out
this message through time and every single rock
of the Mission's walls and palisades.

The number of your enemies
their overwhelming power and cruelty
cannot do more than killing you.
For in all logs of the future
your place of fighting to the death
will become a temple of freedom

when your countrymen, thirsting for it,
will complete what you could not finish.

You can hear the voices of the soldiers at Alamo
looking at their wives and children
taking refuge into the unfinished church
                              of the Mission.
"Wife, save my son!"
And their wives did, looking at the carnage that lasted
only ninety minutes
while the sun was rising over the altar.

"Daughter, save our grandchild!"
I hear my parents voices
while the revolutionaries of my country
                              fighting for freedom
were butchered by my other countrymen who hijacked
the Revolution.

I recall December 1989 in Romania
and those heroes who died
fighting against the internal enemies of the country
in the Revolution that broke out
on December 16th in Timisoara
and continued through January 16th
                              throughout the land.

I neither know the names,
nor the number of those killed.
Nobody knows them,
but we all know that
almost every day
others added their names to that list, in silence.

Silenced, heroes of my country,
I hear your voices in Alamo.

Coming from the East to the West,
with all the sorrows of having lost my battle,
I regain hope by listening to Alamo's message,
delivered to me after one hundred seventy years.

Esperanza's yellow flowers
are all over in bloom in Alamo's courtyard.
Yellow is the color of Hope.
You can see it on Romania's flag, too.

The sun rises over Romania's shrines
and I feel Romania has empowered me
to use my voice and talk to you.

III

NIGHTS

OCTOBER

Commingled Times and Spaces...

Roaming with my literary friends
                through the Village –
as I used to do in my student years –
some from Paris, some from Mexico City, some
from Bucharest, some even based in Queens,
writers in exile or longing to become so,
speaking Romanian on the streets of Soho,
dreaming of subduing the world in all languages,
conquering it in fact, though unwittingly,
happy to learn of this from the youth accompanying me,
who tell about their reactions
                        upon reading the latest book.

At *Olive Tree* by midnight,
I chalk out blooms and battlefields
upon the green granite table.
Times have commingled (and self-obliterated)
                    as spaces have;
the here-and-the-now is buzzing
                in a high-strung state
with hellish peals of laughter coming from the theater
in the basement below.

It's muggy; the ocean air gnaws at the root
                of our thoughts;
fog brings in the deadly sternness of the waves,
as it strolls over our words –

waves and words sharing the same common
denominator. Having stayed up late ...
              A full writing morning squandered ...
Flames and murmurs, half-guessed from the hilarious
shadows, projected on the walls.

God has long ceased to talk to me.
Please, give me a hug.

The sound of life,
        its infinitesimal gurgling
        traverses all the layers of matter
during nights of lovemaking.

Instead of adjusting the range of the canon fire
to reach my world and its average existence,
its ironies, petty jokes, parody, the stable warmth, which
Thomas Mann used to talk about,
the bullshit anyone could understand;
I've leveled it so as to encompass the vanity of eternal art!
The written books are like the charge of the heavy
brigade, sending its fireballs beyond the battlefield.
What's lying beyond that?

I know that sleepless nights lie in store for me,
I do ...

NOVEMBER's Cleaning up Souls ...

Blazing foliage down the streets of New York,
emotions, agony, the foolishness of summer–
November's cleaning up those souls
that will blossom next spring.

Bird callings, unheard before, mixed signals of joy and
pain – While I have experienced them
one by one, in separation.

I blend with the pelicans resting on the trees of South
Seas plantations and sense, in my profound sleep, Key
West's infinitesimal immersion into the ocean.

Taken over by the immemorial instinct
                        of their ancestors,
alligators escape over the fences of reservations,
coming back slowly to the fields of condos
built on the former Everglades swamps.

Flocks of migratory birds replenish
Florida's marshlands, avoiding winter's emotions
whose magnitude might kill
any living being: the amount of pain
opening the wounds of poetry,
sadistically inflicting inspiration.

DECEMBER

What I Have to Find Does Really Exist...

Within walking distance from the shores
                      of the Atlantic,
the Bronx lies under a blanket of snow
like my native village on the Dobrudja steppe,
restrained only by the furies of the Black Sea.

Battling the gusts blowing from Alaska, I'm seeking – as I
was then, over there, withstanding the Crivets that kept
rushing in from the Siberia to snatch me –
this Christmas night, amongst snowdrifts and a pitch-
black snowstorm, the spot above, where the guiding star
has come to a standstill.

The star has risen on high, I know it has,
I'm walking with eyes riveted onto the sky,
under a snowfall muffling Manhattan,
snowflakes instead of stars, peering for the light, gasping
for air, stranded now, as I was then,
surrounded by snowdrifts,
groping down the deserted streets,
        with dogs only barking, as they used to over there,
not knowing either purpose or reason,
carrying about my own storm like the Magi
                      their offerings,
licking the icicles under my brow,
moving forward with the confidence
that what I have to find does really exist
and shall be revealed to me.

JANUARY
On the Eve of the Epiphany

has always been like the immense backbone of destiny
fed by my choices.

Frost-bound cities and forests.
One finally gets lost
in the freezing jungles,
as down wolves' throats.

I've always had an ice-clad tree outside my window
talking to me, in January.

Wrapped in a handmade wool blanket
by my mother's side,
listening to tales whispered by adults
about one, Terente –
the sexiest man on earth
(his penis, in a phenol jar, is displayed at the Natural
History Museum) –
and a thief that managed to escape several times,
but got caught
because of a woman, of course.
This lawbreaker hid himself once
in the Danube everglades,
having mightily enjoyed a poker game
with the village railroad station master,
before the contemplated murder.
He changed his mind, though, upon winning that game,
and vanished into the nearby frost-bound forest.

The screech of ice-bound trees
as their limbs are breaking –

Mother's spirit is abroad again
willing to talk to me –
the same is true of fulfilled prophecies –
a sprig of basil under the pillow,
foretelling, in my dreams, about coming events.

It was the night when I chose exile,
bringing about a cleavage in my life.

Each January I pick exile again,
splintering my own self down its middle
like a cold crevasse leading nowhere.
My Newfoundland is called Mirela –
and its language, Mirelian.
A close kin to Merlinian,
Merlin's idiom.

The icy tree by my window
knows whom I am writing of.

Hours of darkness during which
I find and lose, and find
my love again, on and on –
How many more Januaries
have I to traverse
to achieve fulfillment?

Men never get old; women do—
as it happens when one runs a high temperature:
"I've got only one more penicillin shot
and each kid runs a fever of 105 degrees.

Whom of the two should receive it?"
I hear my father's voice, in my delirium,
a hurtful kind of speeding round
                              a white solid circle.

My brother and I were failing
in a faraway Romanian village,
wrecked in a snowstorm.
To which my mother's sleepless murmur:
"Give to each of them half of it..."

I keep wondering what kind of trees
stood by my windows:
a cherry tree in my childhood,
a poplar during my teenage years.
Now it's one of a nondescript kind
lining a street in Queens, NY –
wintry as all its mates,
its ice-bound branches talking to me
about something I cannot quite make out.

A harsh cold spell overwhelmed the Danube
on the eve of the feast of Epiphany,
freezing it all over, from bank to bank.
A bunch of life convicts would dive naked the next
morning, under the ice, into a hole
which had been dug in it,
seeking to retrieve the crucifix,
cast by a priest,
as part of his blessing of the waters.
The plucky diver that succeeded
in bringing it back
had always been pardoned.

I always used to do my own diving
one January night,
and managed to come back
from under the frozen crust of my choices,
with a new lease of life, which had just been granted.

FEBRUARY

An Elegant Manner of Settling Accounts...

I've been butchering math formulae and metaphors—
all languages, of both Nature's and the World's, are in
$\qquad$ shambles now.
Life looks like an atom
whose nucleus and electrons have been eviscerated.
The Mississippi introduced me
to an elegant manner of settling accounts
during the weary green night
of the hour of the final count.
My specter was invited to the banquet
of the New Orleans ghosts, at a moldy palace.
I'm gliding through the *Mardi Gras* night
alongside the Mississippi toward seas whose anxieties
have been euthanized,
so as to welcome my spectral condition
of body and mind pertaining to another era.
My life's projects have all been fulfilled,
the bottom line was drawn,
all former quarrels fading away
$\qquad$ into the ridiculous.
That wakeful night I felt at a loss
$\qquad$ what other lies to tell,
since the bottle of rum, gulped down
in the Montego Bay, had failed to do the trick.
The Caribbean should have reconciled me
with my own self and eternity.
Yet, here am I at one with the sea,
the Cayman Islands staring out in dismay

at the marine cemetery that has just missed
                                        its prey.
My human atom's filled with more
protons and more electrons than it has ever been.

Northward I ride the ruffled waves,
hurriedly crossing the Mexico Bay,
gliding over the Mississippi marshes
                            through the drizzle,
striking my name off the spectral list
of a New Orleans night club,
sipping a big coffee,
having a dinner to match,
followed by several glasses of Pinot Noir
at my friend the poet's place.
She can't help noticing the discrepancy
between the drained-out discourse of the past
and my present highly enriched human state.
In the French Quarter, on the verge of sleep,
I catch
a whiff of its magnolia trees' electric blossoming.

I breathe the silence in,
aware of the impending storm.

A NIGHT IN MARCH

People and places
can stand me less and less.

I'm dragging night toward day,
saving pieces of it under my eyelids,
struggling with the seconds while crunching it,
devouring the day around its fringes,
reliving events
from the archive of the finest dreams,
walking about in a somnambulist manner
down that noon's streets,
which are still putting up with me.

Changing dreams is still acceptable,
their hues– brighter than ever.
I drink some water and dash back into the dream
shading my eyes against the break of day,
clinging to the edge of night with all my might.
I hate those days that are equal with the nights;
dreams need time to develop;
they can even rout the devil away,
when they crack his paradoxes before the solstice.

Daylight and the endless night I'm carrying inside me –
its sweetness feeding
on the holy sluggishness of March,
when seeds start putting their first roots down.

LATE DAWN IN APRIL

I have delivered myself this year, as it were,
to flesh's selfhood
in the forests of cherry and tulip trees
lining the banks of the Potomac.

The Danube can hardly remember me.

The fragrance of lilies and roses
                no longer intoxicates the air;
the same with the nightingales' song,
                as Mother told me,
whose absence strikes one, in the first place.

The soil is bitter – chilly waves arise from the ongoing
siege of the waters against the city.

One more April night granting the passage.

The limbs of a cherry tree –
more like a silken fabric
shredded in the storms of the centuries –
are holding me
in the swaddling bands of their petals.

I miss my mother's embrace.

Darkness gets whipped up
in the forest of blossoming cherry and tulip trees.

Prophecies haunt

the imperial reservoir –
the city built on marshland.

Blood and pain—
it is not clear which direction I should follow –
death and life seem the same.
Who's going to advise me where to go?

KEEPING TIME IN MAY

Mirela is a person's name built up of three musical notes,
of which "La" – the last one – is the note
the Universe resorts to in talking to us:
the sound Hydrogen goes by.

Mirela was begotten by midnight –
Dawn's memory, as the embodiment of youth,
bears no resemblance to its duskier counterpart.

Mirela does not poke fun at poetry.
She does not crack jokes about it either.
Her thrust aims beyond making an audience laugh—
She refrains from cajoling ambiguities—

Poetry's her realm—not that which might
be labeled fiction, plays, or essays.

The third, the second and the sixth
interval of the diatonic scale—
the last of which "La" underscores the Universe—
engendered a new entity in her mother's womb.

She is constantly singing
arias in La (A), and Re (D) and Mi (E)—
as part of the Universal Symphony
in La (A) Major.
            Mark the way her voice stands out
among the choir of the elements,
as they melodiously accompany her!

Mi and Re are close to Do (C),
the homing C – she's afraid to lose it –
while the distant A pushes toward the limits.

The music obvious in May's wee hours
alleviates the strain of keeping
time for the Symphony
in A (La) Major.

ROMANIAN JUNE

Beauty saved my people in times of terror.

This June, the Romanian soil has put on a purple tint –
                                          self-healing color.

The trees clung with all their might to their blossoms –
a hope that the raging horror
has come to a kind of closure.

In the absence of goodness,
magnificence takes over the land,
                              the minds, and the souls.

It is about that splendor of the green pastures
on which the courageous ones
were butchered while defending their country.

It is the rich sheen of the Carpathian Mountains
where, in those dreadful times,
the brave ones went into hiding,
but were betrayed by their own people
and put to death in those impenetrable forests.

It is the distinctive beauty of the Danube
and the Black Sea –
the shy clouds,
the red geraniums in their window boxes,
the sweet dry air heavy with fragrances –
the June blooming season,
the newly-baked bread,

the softness of moonshine,
the sparkling brooks,
the perfect harmony of colors,
the gentle feel of the sand and riverbeds –
and yet, all over, unfairness seemed
to rule supreme.

It was there that I had been sent
to apprehend beauty.
On account of my loving kindness,
once the learning process was over,
they decreed I was ripe to be destroyed.
Luckily, I could turn to exile as a way out.

The beauty and richness of the land
preserved my people in times of endless horror.

Romania's purplish landscapes are
her inner healing wounds.
The land as such has been chosen,
and so far it has hardly been tested by God,
like everything that He has ever chosen.

JULY'S GIVES AND TAKES

The summer demands and takes away
too much,
But night, the reserved, the reticent, gives more
than it takes.

John Ashbery

To be matchless —
a fairy-tale's trauma.

He looks at her while dancing
and wonders of the matchless
hot and cold of her grace

The paradigm of summer
is the bright nightmare of the imagination.
He enters the breathing slice of life
through the music of prophecies.

Waves of peerless distortions
attack him
as languidly he moves
with the ambiguity of hysteria.

Night will feed you
as a relief from the boiling day's comprehension.
Summer in the desert's summer
         takes everything from you
while night is giving.

Evenings heal the wounds of the sun.
Eyes resist in the first hours of relief.
Fractured words –
one's voice's desperation.

One has been looking for...
Drawers crammed with things ...
The cleaning up of ...
Sleep goes void ...
He forgets how it could ...
The horizon...
the streets ... vanish.

I am in New York now –
the Atlantic, I notice, is breeding the style
of my poetry.

AUGUST

Eluding Mortality

Insomnia adorned by storms
is breathing wonders.
Numbness' lust for happiness!

The loneliness at the heart of all possible worlds.
"I'm a trouble-making girl!" seized by panic
at the thought of starting anything new in my life.
A tiny bit of a delusion this loneliness
which like a coyote followed me
howling all through the desert's mornings.

"No, you're not!" I was told in my dream.

Both sand storm
and sand cloud
crept into my thoughts.
A bird caged
by the desert's winds
may become an angel in search of redemption.

A hot rain is gracefully flooding the desert.

Learn to have fun with mortality
like a gambler in Las Vegas casinos:
the one that gets it all
is least concerned about winning.

SEPTEMBER

The Vortex

I'm peering through gaps inside flashes of lightning.

Whatever's lying beyond the light
has been denied to me.
Waves of vapor shimmer over the hot
mountains, scorpions, thistles, eagles.
I craved for a miracle
and the sky shattered
                      in pursuit of me.

I did not quite manage to dislodge myself
                      to the point of sliding.
I am feeling my way down the other side of the vortex.

I balance in my lap some rowdy slabs
lifted from the lowlands of the Sedona Mountains –
the holy place on this continent
before the advent of the white man.
I'm not looking for an answer,
but for a confirmation
that I'm not aimlessly rambling up and down the heath.

I'm a guide, so I'm told.
Whom do I guide and where to?

I drink cool water from a whirlpool
which springs underneath the stones in my lap,
getting ready for the tough challenge ahead,
involving the huge scale of a new beginning.

Other Books by Mirela Roznoveanu

Published in Romanian—Titles in Translation:

CRITICISM:
-*Modern Readings. Essays*, 1978
-*D. R. Popescu. A Critical Monograph*, 1983
-*The Civilization of the Novel: from Ramayana to Don - Quixote, Vol. I*—1983, *Vol. II*—1991
In Preparation:
-*The Civilization of the Novel: from Ramayana to Don Quixote,* 2nd edition.

FICTION:
-*Always in Autumn*, 1988
-*Life on the Run*, 1997
-*Platonia*, 1999
-*Time of the Chosen*, 1999

POETRY:
-*Apprehending the World,* 1998

Published in English:

ESSAY:
-*Toward a Cyberlegal Culture*, 2001, 2nd edition 2002

FICTION:
-*The Life Manager and Other Stories,* 2004

POETRY:
-*Born Again — in Exile,* 2004